THE

CURRENTS

OF THE

WORLD

THE

CURRENTS

OF THE

WORLD

QUINN BAILEY

Homebound Publications
Ensuring that the mainstream isn't the only stream.

HOMEBOUND PUBLICATIONS

Ensuring the mainstream isn't the only stream

Postal Box 1442, Pawcatuck, Connecticut 06379-1442
www.homeboundpublications.com

Quantity sales and special discounts are available on quantity purchases by corporations, associations, bookstores and others. For details, contact the publisher or visit wholesalers such as Ingram or Baker & Taylor.

ISBN · 978-1-947003-88-0
First Edition
Front Cover Image © Marco Molitor
Interior and Cover Designed by Leslie M. Browning

Printed in the United States of America
10 9 8 7 6 5 4 3 2 1

To those traveling 'round the edge

CONTENTS

THE ONLY TWO DIRECTIONS

This world has only two true directions,
Towards and away.

The big fear, in the end, is to awake and find that
You chose away.

That the hand
Which held you down
Was none other
Than your own.

Remember

The pursuit
Of that which is not truly us
Renders even the most
Powerful vision useless.

Recognize

When the boulder in front of the cave
Begins to shift

When that first illuminating shaft
Pierces the dark

Do not hesitate long

Do not waste time
Anticipating the griefs
Yet to come.

They cannot be helped and perhaps are necessary

On that long
And awkward walk
Towards yourself.

CARRYING COALS

I think often of the before times
When we roamed in
Small bands and fire
Was our constant companion.

Of those diligent keepers
Who, though the wind and rain
Was indifferent
And the prowling uncertainties
Lurked always in the darkness

And at times even
The dream of warmth
Seemed forbidden,

Carried with them
That little glow,
Tenderly wrapped in a nest
Of barks and mosses,

Just waiting for
That steady hand,
That patient breath,
To bring us back to life.

THE CURRENTS OF THE WORLD

You are adrift
Floating on a vast ocean, clinging to your little piece
Of the wreckage for what could have been forever.

Until one day,
As you crest yet another wave
It is there in the distance.

How did you not see it before?
Has it always been there?
Softly calling your name.

You turn and for the first time in your life kick!

Fighting against the swell. Fighting until your muscles burn
And your own name means nothing!

But you get no closer.

So you keep fighting
Your piece of that long forgotten shipwreck
Held up like a shield,
You fight until the saltwater
Mixes with the blood
In your mouth

And you wish your bones
Would just break already!

Still you are no closer.

It is in that moment you realize
If you wish to continue you must let go
Of that which has kept you safe,
On the surface, all these years.

With the deepest gratitude you slip below
And let the currents of the world
Take you.

THE CARVER'S HANDS
-For Walter-

Even at rest
The old carver's hands
Look how one might hope
For their god's hands to look.

Never rushed, but ready always
To take up again
That impossible blade
That opens the door to his craft.

A rough alchemy
Of wood and metal
And shape,

Each pass deliberate
In its takings and leavings,

Each cut quick and precise,
The chips falling
Easy as time
Into piles on the floor.

Each curl of wood
An offering
To that form
Still being found

THIS SPLENDID SHAPE

And like that it was done.
You stepped out
Of the life you knew
And into the life
You had banished yourself from.

And though it felt like defeat
To say it out loud
And it felt like loneliness to leave,
You did.

Only now, outside that decaying house,
Can you see it
For what it truly was.

The perfect cocoon,
Each privilege, each deprivation,
Carefully crafted
To make you
This splendid shape.

WATCHING SALMON

In the river dark shapes
Carve the depths.
Patiently shifting
Against the current
Always moving
Always back
Towards the source.

Even as death approaches
And the body,
Soon to be outgrown,
Decays, still their cold
Eyes speak with joy
Of the scent of home
Pulling louder and louder.

DREAM HUNT

One night it will just pass
Plain in the firelight.

That thing you've been
Hunting for so long,
Suddenly right in front of you,
Unafraid.

As if everything,
The cunning traps,
The dogged trailing,
Was all just for show.

Some elaborate ceremony
Of the inevitable.

And now this

No desperate chase,
No revelatory
Final showdown,

Just a gentle meeting of eyes,
A shared moment of stillness
And a slow turning to fade
Back into the night.

A LIFE FOR MINE

She is taken easily into my arms,
Her body full and soft, tucked under
An elbow, as I settle into the chair
Over the bucket.

On my lap,
The apron corners secured
Against any thought of escape,
Her head sticks out
Past my knees and I pause

Seeing her brand new.

The orange eye shiny
And open to the world,
Her feathers smooth and shifting with each breath.
A reverence for the grace of her design slows me
Even as the ancient necessity of hunger
Urges me on.

From here everything is thank you.
Thank you.

The knife, sharp as a key, in one
Hand, the other pulls her neck long
Revealing the pale skin underneath.

I rest there the flat-back of the blade
Moving it slowly
Like a violin bow settling
Into a familiar song.

Until, no longer afraid
Of this new sensation,
Her eyes close,
Her breath steadies,
And it is time.
In one fierce motion
The blade is flipped,
The song is ended.

Her neck opens like a warm river
Flowing over my hands longer than expected,
The last waves of her heart crashing into
The white bucket at my feet
Until a final shiver runs
The length of her body
Or mine and I know
Without a doubt
There is a soul
And it has left.

AWAKE

Awake gently if you can.
Like an infant tossed joyfully
Into the soft devastation
Of knowing exactly where you are,

To be awake in this world
Is to be betrayed beautifully.

To learn to stand alone knowing that everyone
You've ever loved or ever will love has nothing
You can actually keep.

But like the moth or the matchstick
You must love.

You must love what makes you feel small,
Welcome it.
It is the surest path
To those forgotten parts
So desperately needed.

To be awake is to say I have been disfigured
Into something
I was not ready to be
But I will not lie

In the doorway,
Like some broken thing,
Waiting for the cold comfort of death.

I have built a fire
From the wet wood of this heart,
I have taken up the crown at my feet.

Because our only hope is with those
Who like the seed,
Can hold and be held.
Like the waves,
Can move and be moved.
Like the dreamer, can awake
And continue to dream.

Our only hope is to trust
In each other's dreams.

WHAT IF

-For Laura-

I do not know if
The trees can speak,

I do not know if I
Have the ears to hear them.

But what if they can?
What if we could?

What would it be then
To walk out into
That wonderfully
Uncultivated choir

As the slow honeyed
Voices of the trees filled
The valley with their
Strange harmonies,

And the only thing we had
To do was stand with
The other living things
Of the world
And listen.

AFTER THE NEWS

It is hard
Not to think
Surely this all
Will crumble
And every step will be called
Progress.

Take heart
You, who feel so alone
In this world
On fire

Hope is not hopeless

Every day
We find each other
More and more.

THE REMINDER

We all stopped
Early on that Friday morning
To let the family of deer through.
A small heard,
No more then twenty
In both lanes, we sat still on the road
With no protest to get back
To our busy day.
As the mother and her two yearlings
Made, in that hesitant
And then hurried
Gait of uncertainty,
Their shy way across
The road.
Surely they had seen, as I had,
The bodies
Of their kin snagged and twisted
On the banks of this impassible river.
I wonder if she felt,
As I did
A small victory, as
Her meager dynasty
Slipped into the caves of
The blackberry thicket

And we strangely
Satisfied let the current
Push us on.

THE DESIRE OF TONIGHT

The night moves, the house creaks
Already the trees are dancing

Wild on the hill and the drumming rain
Will not be stopped.

Outside the restless wind calls,
Patiently waiting to undress you.

It is late!

Step out of whatever failing shelter
You have found.

Tonight surrender is your shield, not to quake and cower behind,
But to step with unwavering into battle.

To find the fierceness and the softness
That is required of a real life.

To feel fully each deep needle
Of the heart.

For only willingly laid upon the altar
Do we see how each blow is a gift

And so make a dance of
Our fearful stumblings.

THE BETWEEN PLACE

The shoreline stretches on
A between place
A meeting place
You must walk there.

Be warned no bearing can be taken here,
No course plotted through the swirling pools
Here waypoints fade into the mist
and the sweeping hand of the tide
Leaves nothing with which to find your way back.

Yes the solidness of the ground will tempt you
With promises of certainty
And the waves will pull at you
Like a lover in the night
Whispering

Come…drift into me.

But you must walk the middle way.

Where success and failure become obsolete,
Where the boundary-holders of the mind are lulled to sleep
By the steady rhythm of your own heart
And the great cliff faces are cracked and sheared,
Revealing their ancient lines.

In this place true names

Are whispered on the breeze

And the delicate seeds of newness

Are washed ashore

Begging to be carried into the world.

THE DARK WATER

The dark water is waiting

Cool and still
In the deep places
You abandoned long ago.
Forgotten in a lifelong youth
Of breathing fire
Where all you cared about was roaring empty things.

The dark water is waiting

Now that some gold has been sifted
From the maggot box,
Now that you move with deliberate broken steps
And the scars you once tried to hide
Have become your map.

The dark water is waiting

Not as the burden
You thought you had to bear
For so many miles
Through the endless cracked hills
But as the weight that keeps you steady
On the soft green earth.

THE WITCH

Beware the witch
Her faces are many.
You will know her
By the smell of roses
And little deaths.

Her strange divinity
Will surely peel back your skin,
Rub you in the dirt of the earth
And leave you
Hanging upside down
In the pines to rot awhile.

Like some broken bell
In an old church tower you will wait
Silent on the hill
The stars burning
Brighter and brighter each night.

Until one day,
When the right beam breaks,
All the kingdoms
Of the forest will pause

And the heavy masks
Of falseness will slip from you
With such a sound!

Then what royalty you could be.

THE RUNNER

It comes suddenly
Hornets in the heels
Bursting from the peaks above
With a grace that mocks speed.

Shouting "There is more than this for you!"
More than the casting of nets into dry rivers

More than the slow decay of repetition
     More than the slow decay of repetition
       More than the slow decay of repetition

Then feet, that might be your own,
Spark the night like flint
Pounding along the granite ridgeline
And just as suddenly it is gone

Leaving tiny black constellations
That lingering behind your eyelids.
The only sign that everything
For you has changed.

ANCIENT CONVERSATIONS

Rise early while the day is still soft
While the birds gently call the sun
Up over the mountains.

The misty tide recedes
Leaving its delicate treasures
Hanging from each needle

And downturned blade.
Countless rough-cut jewels,
Slowly dissolving back into the earth.

This and a thousand other ancient conversations
Are happening all around us always
The only payment asked is our attention.

VISION TWIN

Maybe none of us come
Into this world alone.
Maybe we each have a vision twin
A remembering that enters just ahead of us
Knowing we are not ready to follow.

Maybe as we grow it is waiting
Just around the corner, leaving compasses
Disguised as dark flocks of birds,
Maps coded into the creek beds and
Bone piles of our youth.

Blurry snapshots
That hint at a true shape.

Maybe later it is like a shadow.
Always at our heels, the whisper at the edge
Of the fire's glow, seen only when
We willingly turn away from the light
And even then only for a moment.

Maybe there is no guarantee
Of a reunion. The weight we carry
Is heavy and hard to find, the road is long,
And important things can fill a lifetime.

But maybe when your heart begins speaking
Words your mouth can't yet make,
You will not ignore it.

The feather, the key, the offering
Left at your doorstep.

Maybe together, on shaky legs, you'll stumble
Out into that delicate waiting world
Just to see what you can rattle.

TWO HEARTS

Two hearts beat inside my chest.
Two sinewy wrestlers tumbling around
The soft pink arena of my ribcage.

One,
The desire for freedom,
To not be held down
By the nets of a comfortable life
Where big dreams stay buried in the clay.

The other,
The longing for the steady rhythm of settling.
For the constant and the reliable,
Where more delicate flowers
Can root and bloom.

Two hearts
Are all I've ever known
Their contrary beats weaving in and out
Like bats in the deep blue of the evening,
Drawn to things only they can perceive.

But always,
As the light fades away and I

Returning to my little cave, hear
between the beats, a quiet voice
That remembers all the things
 I don't have to be.

SING

Maybe our job
Is that of the
Birds

Simply to collect
The soft things
Of the world

And sing about it.

THE HIBERNATING TIMES

Old Ice Bear Den Blanket Burrow
Red Coals Window Frost Kettle Steam
Frozen Road Night Walk Loose Time

Bear Time

Asked about you.

It wants to know
If you have given up
"Have to" and "not enough"

They say the well of dreams is deep
And will not dip itself.

BENEATH THE ARMOR

Beneath the armor you've
Often called home, and
Preservation, and necessary as skin

Waits a sensuous body
Asking to be anointed with all the
Sweet nectar of this life.

For you to surrender
That polished shell, formed tightly
Over fears of owing the world anything,

And rise up spinning,
Like some holy dancer,
Into arms you never knew
Were waiting just for you.

LOVE, THE BUTTERFLY, AND THE WINDOW

As the storm rolls in
The ragged butterfly knocks
With its whole being
At the window.
Each labored act,
Soft as eyelashes
On a cheek, its last.

We arrive
Colors faded,
Wings frayed,
Seeking shelter from that
Which has always
Confused
And halted us.
Hoping doubtfully
For a safe place to land.

Love arrives
Small and
Doubtful
And worn
Asking softly,
Over the racket
Of routine,
What truly is
The cost of
Opening?

THE DOOR HAS MANY FORMS

It is there,
Waiting for you
Just beyond the thick
Skirt of the trees
Or half way 'round
The edge of the always pregnant
Pond. A place not hidden
Though only you
Can find it. A place that
Asks nothing of you
Though, you could
Give it everything.

Once there, a part
Of you will never leave.
Like the long silvery line
Of a spider sailing out
On the breeze it will stay with you
As you climb the endless
Necessary steps, and hurry
Through the sharply lit tunnels.

It will be there
Like the hawk on the streetlight,
Like the yarrow in the vacant lot,

A reminder
That the door
Has many forms.

A TINY WARMTH

I am just a baby bird,
Helpless and frail.
Held above the aggressions of the world
By a nest I had no part in making.

A tiny warmth buried in the fluff,
Calling out my needs
In a constant, shrill voice.
For so long I resented it.
Meticulously dismantling
Each nest that was given to me.

So afraid of my own innocence
I would plummet from
The branches of the familiar
Down to the unforgiving ground,
Again and again,
Resisting what I was
To grasp at what I should be.

But even the unforgiving
Holds us, the free fall
Protects us,
And the hard ground
Is a nest in its own way.

Now, as I nestle deeper, I rejoice
Knowing there is strength
In the need for soft things,
Songs of beauty in each
Cry for nourishment,
And the grace of flight
Hidden in surrender.

THE EXCAVATION OF A HEART

The excavation of a heart is lonely work
Though you might not have known it at first.

Looking to others to fill that ragged jigsaw hole
In your chest.

But after so many you know how the body mutinies
What the heart is not behind.

So now, though the insufficiencies
Of childhood were great

And the patterns of dysfunction
Feel etched into

The very geography of your body,
You have started to dig.

Through a history of Self-mummification,
Through all the reasons
To not save your own life.

Down into that low sediment,
That dark rich soil
Who knows what you might find.

Maybe a chest
Thumping with the song
Of your own wild heart.

DANCE YOUR ANIMAL

Dance your animal
Dance with tooth and
Claw and fur and feather.
Dance in the woods
Behind your house
Or in the back alley
With the broken glass
Dance for the hope,
Dance for the loss,
Dance on your knees
For all the nights
Of pain squandered
Pretending it was all okay.
Dance for the good and
Dance for the bad.
Dance for the beauty
In all the parts
That nobody wanted.
Dance for the small things
Dance for the healing
Dance, Dance, Dance.
Until your sweat
Runs shimmering lines
Down your body

And each step howls
Like a blessing
To the necessary surrender
Of motion.

STORIES

You know all the
Moving things
Murmur tales that
Would terrify and excite
If only we knew
How to listen.

You cry I am broken
And I am comfortable
And would never dare
But the world is woven
On a loom
Of broken things and
Each thread will be tested.

We all have felt, at times,
The unrelenting push of bigger wheels
Turning through our lives.

Asking will you trust,
Knowing what you do of how
The world treats those
Who would be free.

Will you trust with both hands
Those unmerciful hammers
Shaping us
Blow by blow
Into stories needing to be told.

THE LAUGHING REVOLUTION

The revolution starts on Sunday and it will be nothing
Like you planned.
So bring loved ones and unloved ones,
Bring all that you can.
Bring privilege and shame and sharp knives for cutting
Bring spices, and sweetgrass and strong ropes for lashing
Bring anguish and music, bring feathers and seeds
Bring art and arrows and un-negotiable needs,
Bring all the things people don't want to see
Bring rain and lightning and the long summer days
Bring alchemy and animals, and dogs for the hunt
Bring fools, and witches, and the ghosts no one sees
Bring lovers and haters and holy mess makers
Bring drummers, fiddlers, and fine shoes for dancing
Bring faith and courage and whiskey in jars
Bring flowers, and blankets, and cornmeal for the dead
Bring tea and candles and good songs for walking
But most of all bring laughter
We will need it before this night is out.

LOSING MY EDGE

Where does it end really?
Me I mean.
Sure there is this skin
Soft and stretched like a drum
Over this bone frame.

But lying here in the dark
It only takes one breath, one beat,
And I am cascading out of myself
Spilling on to the sheets and across the floor
Saturating the walls until this whole
House sighs with me.

Soon the frogs outside start singing
And that is me too,
Half in the mud,
The glassy black water
Rippling with each
Call for a companion.

And why not this whole forest,
Tall elders swaying with deep laughter.

Or this whole river valley
Cutting slowly through the meadowlands
And out to the sea.

And why not the whole living earth,
Half-wrapped in its tattered
Cloak of night,
Warming itself by a dying fire
In an endless dark.

TRUST IN THE SOIL

All growth starts in the dark.

So often desperate for any sign
Of life

We uncover too soon that which needs
To stay buried.

A good gardener knows all things seek the light
In their own time.

A good gardener knows how to trust in the soil.

ENOUGH

It will never be enough.
Know that now.
Each moment of satisfaction passes
As does the rest.

Enduring as the clouds
Already shifting overhead,
And you are left with what?

More useful fictions
To embolden you up
The next false peak.

Who you want to be
Is a distraction.

Who you are
Cannot be named
By any shape
The mouth can make.

IN SEASON

1.

There is a tumbling.

The bay is alive and the field

Above it too.

Grey winds moving across the

Open water and stiff brown stalks alike.

Land and sea,

So different in nature

But in this moment

Lovers Caught in

The same rough tempest.

2.

There is a stillness.

Snow lying heavy on the branch,

The upper world gone quiet

The light having vanished on a sudden slack tide.

Even the trees have retreated into their

Deep repose to dream of

Next years blossoms.

3.

There is a quickening.

As the sun touches again

The waiting faces of the plant world

We humans feel the warm

Heartbeat of the earth
Stirring in us. That sharp
Desire to find each other
And unravel our bodies,
Evaporating into that
Ancient horizon of desire.

4.

There is a settling.
The meadow
Sun soaked and still
Except for the lazy hymns of the insects
Pulsing through the shimmering heat.
In this slow love song
It is easy to find a thousand ways
To say, I love you.

THE VALLEY OF THE MOON

Thick, the fog turns
The morning sun into a bright
Shimmering moon.

The trees emerge like
Long spectral hands
Out of the bone white veil.

The hawk sits
Like a sooty diamond,
Waiting to be polished

On the coarse grit
Of its prey.

OUT HERE

Walking
When done right
Is mostly listening
With steps in between.

Stopping to be still long enough
That it feels like
Treason to start again.

Who am I to break this silence.
That is the job of Wren,
Or the Thrush,
Or the creaking Firs.

I am just a visitor here.

Each crunching step confirms
My citizenship to a different world,
A made world of quickness and improvement.

Out here that is all far away.

Out here it is still understood
You cannot improve fresh snow,
Or the glittering throat of the hummingbird,
Or these maple seeds, like angels of spring,
Falling slowly to the ground.

OUR TINY VESSEL

This is no dress rehearsal.
Know that each of us
Is woven together.

Each a thread that if
Allowed to be frayed
Or broken, will loosen
The weave and lessen the world.

The hermit crabs ,
Amidst the turbulent rocks
Show so much
Faith in letting go.

The flocks of geese
Working the sky southward,
A trust in the call home.

It takes both
To say I will begin again
To play my part

In this messy and merciful world.
And to try and do it
With something close to humility.

For even as our tiny vessel
Sets out upon the ocean

Teeming with gods waiting to test us,

So does a great wind
Hurry from across the world
To fill our sail.

I AM A FORGOTTEN REBELLION

Stopped alone in the dark
The street's scaled black back shines
Wet and slithering from the rain.

The furry engine rattles, revs, and settles
As above me two eyes, glowing red
In the empty darkness, stare at the
Bold mouse caught in its unblinking gaze.

How easy it would be to accelerate
Into that waiting abyss.
The open mouth of this sudden
Fierce guardian of the crossroads.

Would it somehow
Make up for all
The wasted time, and
The trivial nothings of life

To claim a little rebellion
On this rainy city night.

But before the uncoiling of caution
And muscle, the towering serpent
Blinks green and with no witness
To stop me, I scurry on.

The invitations wet reflection
Nothing more then blurry diamonds
Growing smaller and smaller
In the rearview.

WOUND

Tell where you
Are wounded
Pull it apart

Again and again
Stick your finger in
The slippery mess

Find what was severed
And you find
What is sacred to you.

SLEEPING IN THE FIELD

The stars shine tonight
With a new urgency
And I am in love
With each one.

That adolescent breaking
At the seams,
Electricity burning out
my bones,
Can't take my eyes off you,
Except for when
You're around,

Kind of love.
It is good practice sometimes
Loving this way
Something so distant.

PRAISE

Praise now your body
Laid out before me like
A contoured map
Of the divine
Waiting to be explored.

Praise now our bones
Humming like the pale northern
Moon on a cold clear night.

Praise now the fire
In the caves of our hearts
Burning against all that would submit us.

Praise now the pattern
That persists in
Each pinecone as in
Each galaxy.

Praise now the mistakes
That with difficulty
Have shown the path.

Praise now the two threads
Knit together in the soft
Temple of our mothers.

Praise now the darkness
That hides us and
Resides in us.

SOMETHING IS FISHING FOR YOU

The hook dressed just right
To catch your eye,
Each movement
Artfully performed to stir
A buried hunger.

Patiently, the line thin
And strong waits,
Knowing you will fight
Knowing you will do
Almost anything

To not be pulled up
From the murky depths
To not be wrenched at last
Into the sharp glittering world
Where you will lie gasping
In amazement at what has
Always been.

TIDELINE

Is there any
Greater healer
Then being licked clean
By the salty tongue of the ocean.

No offering once
Given to that
Rolling watery jaw
Can stay jagged for long.

This mosaic of smoothed
Stones and glass
Are a testament to that

You are no exception.

ALL WAS GOOD IN THE KINGDOM

All was good
In the kingdom.
Until one day,
A truth of yourself was discovered
And you woke up
In tattered rags,
Stumbling upon the dusty road,
The gates barred shut behind you.

For awhile you remained,
Stagnant, clawing at the mortar and
Kicking up dust
With desperate cries for justice.

But finally, hands bleeding and throat dry,
You crawled into the woods
And truly got lost.

There among the dark trees
The small rituals
Of the rains found you and
The mossy hands
Of the mountains
Performed their
Gentle surgery

And all the ways you
Had been asking for help
Could finally be heard.

Now on callused feet
The night wrapped around you
Like an old friend.
You slip softly
From door to darkened door
Down the paved empty streets

To whisper under windows
Of those still asleep-
Don't wake up at the end
Of someone else's life.

ACKNOWLEDGMENT

My deepest gratitude to all that has supported me and continues to support me. Thank you to all my friends and family for encouraging me to continue to write and share my poetry. Thank you to all the story keepers, myth tellers, and poets who have gone before me. Thank you to all the wild beings and places whose secrets continue to inspire me.

ABOUT THE AUTHOR

Quinn Bailey is a poet, naturalist, and wildlife tracker who for the last seven years has been helping people find a deeper connection to the natural world through ancestral skills such as bird language, wilderness living, and cultural mentoring. Growing up between Orcas Island, Washington and Big Sur, California, he discovered a strong sense of belonging and curiosity about the natural world and feels most at home wandering the wooded hills and rocky shores surrounding the Salish Sea where he now lives.

HOMEBOUND PUBLICATIONS
POETRY OFFERINGS

———

Joy is the Thinnest Layer by Gunilla Norris

Ruminations at Twilight by L.M. Browning

Having Listened by Gary Whited

Four Blue Eggs by Amy Nawrocki

The Uncallused Hand by Walker Abel

Rolling Up the Sky by Linda Flaherty Haltmaier

Water, Rocks and Trees by James Scott Smith

To Look Out From by Dede Cummings

The School of Soft-Attention by Frank LaRue Owen

After Following by Burt Bradley

A Taste of Water and Stone by Jason Kirkey

Children to the Mountain by Gary Lindorff

Night, Mystery & Light by J.K. McDowell

Rooted & Risen by Timothy P. McLaughlin

Blood Moon by Andrew Jarvis

WWW.HOMEBOUNDPUBLICATIONS.COM
LOOK FOR OUR TITLES WHEREVER BOOKS ARE SOLD